MW01602011

BECOMING UNSH

Rediscovering the Woman You Were Always Meant to Be

Realigned. Rediscovered. Empowered to Lead.

by Tongie Davis

© 2025 Axis North Coaching, LLC

For permissions or inquiries:
info@AxisNorthCoaching.com

Published by Axis North Coaching, LLC •
www.AxisNorth.org

Dedication

To my husband, Anthony — thank you for your unwavering love, support, and belief in me. Your steady encouragement gave me the space and strength to bring this vision to life.

To every woman who has shared her story, her prayers, and her courage — you inspired these pages.

And to God — the true Author of every aligned step — may this work honor You in every heart it reaches.

Table of Contents

Introduction – The Power of Realignment

There are moments in life when everything familiar begins to shift — when titles fade, roles change, and the version of yourself that once fit so perfectly no longer feels like home. For many women, this happens quietly, somewhere between what was and what's next. I know that space well. It's the in-between — a sacred pause where God invites us to listen, to realign, and to rediscover who we've always been in Him.

When I found myself in that place, I asked God, "What's next?" The answer didn't come as a roadmap but as a whisper: "Be still and realign."

Realignment begins with surrender — not striving. It's the gentle turning of the heart back toward true north, where Christ becomes our compass. When we stop forcing direction and start seeking alignment, peace returns. Confidence grows. Purpose awakens.

This book was born out of that realignment. It's a guide, a conversation, and an invitation. Over the next chapters, you'll walk through the same process that changed my life — rediscovering identity, restoring confidence, and reigniting purpose.

We'll dig deep, pray honestly, and grow boldly. Some chapters will feel like healing; others will feel like stretching. But every page will point you back to the truth: you are still becoming, and in Him, you are unshakable.

As you journey through this book, remember — your second act isn't a lesser version of your story; it's the continuation of God's glory through you.

Welcome to your realignment.

Chapter 1 – Identity Reset: Who Am I Now?

"Before I formed you in the womb I knew you, before you were born I set you apart." – Jeremiah 1:5

There comes a point when every woman asks the question, "Who am I now?" After children are grown, careers evolve, or life's rhythm shifts, it's easy to feel as though identity has slipped through your hands. Yet, God never loses sight of who you are. Your assignment may change, but your essence in Him remains.

When God spoke to Jeremiah, He reminded him that identity begins long before birth. The same is true for you—your name, purpose, and gifts were written in heaven before you took your first breath. Realignment begins when you remember who authored your life.

Release the Labels

The world loves labels: mother, employee, caretaker, survivor. Some honor us; others confine us. But God never defined you by a role—He called you His. It's time to release the labels that limit you and embrace the truth that your identity is anchored in Christ, not circumstances.

Rewrite Your Inner Narrative

Many of us live according to outdated stories—chapters written by fear, failure, or expectation. The Kingdom woman learns to edit those narratives with truth. Renewal happens every time you replace "I'm not enough" with "I am chosen."

Identity and Purpose Work Together

When identity is unclear, purpose feels distant. But as identity comes into focus, purpose follows. Before God sends you, He settles you.

Journal Moments

1. Describe a season when you felt uncertain about who you were. What helped you navigate it?

2. Write three truths from Scripture that declare your worth in Christ.

3. Pray and ask the Holy Spirit to reveal any false identities you've carried.

4. Finish this sentence: "God calls me ..."

I am realigned. I am rediscovered. I am empowered to lead.

Chapter 2 – Core Values & Alignment: Living What Matters Most

"Seek first the Kingdom of God and His righteousness, and all these things will be added to you." – Matthew 6:33

Life is full of shifting priorities. For years, you may have lived by what was urgent, not what was important. But the aligned woman knows peace comes when her decisions reflect her deepest convictions. Alignment isn't about perfection — it's about congruence between what you believe, what you value, and how you live.

When Jesus told us to seek first the Kingdom, He gave the blueprint for aligned living: let what matters to God shape what matters to you.

Identify Your True North

Your True North represents your God-given direction — the point your soul faces when you live from purpose rather than pressure. Values may shift across seasons; growth requires reevaluation.

When Values Drift

Misalignment often starts subtly — a small compromise here, a neglected boundary there. Peace is the sign you're walking in alignment.

Kingdom Alignment in Everyday Life

Alignment shows up in your calendar, your finances, your relationships, and your words.

Journal Moments

1. List the three areas of your life that feel out of sync. What small changes could restore balance?

2. Describe what peace feels like to you — emotionally, spiritually, and physically.

3. What boundaries do you need to strengthen to live by your core values?

4. What daily habit would support alignment this week?

My values honor God. My steps reflect purpose. My life is in divine order.

Chapter 3 – Emotional Intelligence & Healing: Mastering the Inner Dialogue

"Above all else, guard your heart, for everything you do flows from it." – Proverbs 4:23

Every thought, every feeling, and every reaction has a root. Emotional intelligence

begins when we start to identify that root rather than simply react to the fruit. For the Kingdom woman, emotional maturity is not the absence of emotion — it's the alignment of emotion with God's truth.

When you guard your heart, you don't shut it down; you steward it. You become aware of what influences your feelings, and you choose responses that reflect wisdom rather than wounds.

Awareness Before Action

The emotionally intelligent woman asks, "Why am I feeling this?" before she decides, "What should I do about this?"

Healing the Hidden Hurts

Many of us carry unhealed places from past relationships, losses, or disappointments. Emotional healing doesn't erase the past — it redeems it.

The Voice Within

Our inner dialogue can either be a battlefield or a sanctuary. Every time you align your thoughts with Scripture, you silence the lies.

Journal Moments

1. Write about a recent situation that triggered strong emotion. What belief or past wound might be connected to it?

2. List three Scriptures that speak to emotional peace.

3. What practices help you regulate emotion — prayer, journaling, walking, breathing?

4. Ask God: "What are You teaching me through what I feel?"

I am healed. I am whole. I am emotionally aligned with the heart of God.

Chapter 4 – Confidence & Voice: Speaking Life

"Death and life are in the power of the tongue." – Proverbs 18:21

Your voice is your instrument of influence. For years you may have quieted it—out of politeness, fear, or habit—but alignment calls you to speak again. Confidence is not volume; it's certainty that what you carry is valuable and necessary.

When God asked Moses to speak, Moses said, "I am not eloquent." God's reply was simple: "Who made your mouth?" The same God who gave you words will fill them with grace and power.

Speaking Life Over Yourself

Words shape worlds. Begin with your own. Stop rehearsing defeat and start declaring destiny.

Boldness in Action

Confidence grows through movement. Step out, even trembling, and courage will meet you there.

Journal Moments

1. When have you felt your voice wasn't heard? How might God redeem that?

2. Write three phrases of life you will speak over yourself daily.

3. Pray aloud for boldness today.

I am confident. I am courageous. I am called to speak life.

Chapter 5 – Purpose & Next Chapter: Becoming Who You're Called to Be

"For we are God's workmanship, created in Christ Jesus to do good works, which God prepared in advance for us to do." – Ephesians 2:10

Purpose isn't found — it's remembered. It was placed in you before time began. When seasons shift, purpose may look different, but its essence remains. God never wastes experience; He weaves it into calling.

From Waiting to Walking

Many women stall because they're waiting for clarity when God is waiting for obedience. Start where you are with what you have; movement invites momentum. "Commit to the Lord whatever you do, and He will establish your plans."

Journal Moments

1. What dreams keep resurfacing no matter how often you dismiss them?

2. How could your life experience bless another woman walking behind you?

3. Pray: Lord, align my gifts with Your purpose and make my next steps clear.

I am purposeful. I am ready. I am becoming who I am called to be.

Chapter 6 — Integration & Activation: Living Aligned

"Let your light so shine before others, that they may see your good works and glorify your Father in heaven." — Matthew 5:16

Alignment without action is theory. This chapter invites you to integrate all you've discovered — identity, values, healing, confidence, and purpose — into daily rhythms.

The Aligned Lifestyle

Morning realignment, midday check-ins, and evening reflection build holy consistency.

Kingdom Activation

God didn't realign you just for reflection — He realigned you for impact.

Journal Moments

1. Where can your obedience create change in your family, community, or church?

2. What two daily rhythms will you implement this week to live aligned?

I am aligned. I am active. I am walking in purpose with unshakable faith.

Chapter 7 – Redefining Success: From Worldly Metrics to Kingdom Impact

"But seek first his kingdom and his righteousness, and all these things will be given to you as well." – Matthew 6:33

For decades, you may have measured success by titles, income, recognition, or accomplishments. But Kingdom success looks different. It's measured in obedience, faithfulness, love, and the fruit of the Spirit that grows in you and through you.

The world celebrates what can be seen; God celebrates what happens in secret. When you shift your definition of success from external validation to internal transformation, peace floods your soul.

The Trap of Comparison

Social media, careers, and even church culture can create false benchmarks. But your assignment is unique to you. Comparing your chapter seven to someone else's chapter twenty steals your joy and clouds your vision.

What Does God Call Successful?

Scripture is clear: success in God's eyes is faithfulness. "Well done, good and faithful servant" (Matthew 25:23) — not "well done, good and famous servant." When you steward what He gives you with integrity and love, you succeed.

Rewriting Your Metrics

Create new measures of success rooted in Kingdom values:

- Am I growing in love?

- Am I walking in obedience?

- Am I using my gifts to serve others?

- Is my life bearing spiritual fruit?

Journal Moments

1. What worldly definitions of success have you carried that no longer serve you?

2. How would your life look different if faithfulness became your primary measure?

3. Write three Kingdom-centered goals for this season.

4. Pray: Lord, help me see success through Your eyes, not the world's.

I am successful in God's eyes. I am faithful. I am fruitful.

Chapter 8 – The Power of Rest: Embracing the Sabbath Rhythm

"Come to me, all you who are weary and burdened, and I will give you rest." – Matthew 11:28

Rest is not laziness; it's obedience. God instituted the Sabbath as a gift, not a burden. Yet many Kingdom women struggle to rest, believing their worth is tied to their productivity. But you are a human being, not a human doing.

When you rest, you declare trust in God's provision. You acknowledge that He is God, and you are not. Rest restores your soul, renews your strength, and realigns your focus.

Why We Resist Rest

Fear often masquerades as busyness. We fear that if we stop, everything will fall apart. But Psalm 127:2 reminds us, "In vain you rise early and stay up late, toiling for food to eat — for he grants sleep to those he loves."

Creating Sacred Pauses

Rest doesn't only mean sleep. It includes:

- Sabbath days set apart for worship and restoration

- Margin in your schedule for breathing room

- Saying no to protect your peace

- Quiet time with God without an agenda

The Fruit of Rest

When you rest well, you work better. Clarity comes. Creativity flows. Compassion grows. Rest is not the absence of work; it's the foundation for sustainable work.

Journal Moments

1. What keeps you from resting fully?

2. How can you build rhythms of rest into your weekly schedule?

3. What does a "Sabbath day" look like for you personally?

4. Ask God: What am I afraid will happen if I rest?

I am allowed to rest. I am restored in His presence. I am renewed for my calling.

Chapter 9 – Stewarding Your Story: Turning Pain Into Purpose

"And we know that in all things God works for the good of those who love him, who have been called according to his purpose." – Romans 8:28

Your story — every chapter, even the broken ones — is part of God's redemptive plan. The pain you've walked through is not wasted; it's preparation. When stewarded well, your story becomes a bridge for someone else's healing.

God doesn't erase our past; He redeems it. The woman who has been healed becomes the healer. The one who has been delivered becomes the deliverer. Your testimony is your ministry.

Owning Your Narrative

You cannot steward what you refuse to acknowledge. Healing begins when you stop hiding your story and start seeing it through the lens of grace. Your scars are proof of survival, not shame.

Sharing With Wisdom

Not everyone deserves your full story, but someone needs the part of it that will set them free. Share strategically, prayerfully, and with boundaries that honor your peace.

The Power of Testimony

Revelation 12:11 says, "They triumphed over him by the blood of the Lamb and by the word of their testimony."

Your voice carries authority when it declares what God has done.

Journal Moments

1. What part of your story have you been reluctant to share? Why?

2. How has God redeemed something painful in your life?

3. Who might benefit from hearing your testimony?

4. Pray: Lord, give me courage to steward my story for Your glory.

My story is not over. My pain has purpose. My testimony will sct others free.

Chapter 10 – Building Kingdom Relationships: Connection Over Perfection

"Therefore encourage one another and build each other up, just as in fact you are doing." – 1 Thessalonians 5:11

Aligned women need aligned community. Relationships rooted in authenticity, accountability, and encouragement create the environment where faith flourishes. But many women settle for surface-level connections because vulnerability feels risky.

Kingdom relationships are different. They prioritize depth over popularity, truth over comfort, and growth over gossip. When you surround yourself with women who call you higher, you become unshakable.

The Danger of Isolation

Isolation convinces you that you're alone in your struggles. It whispers, "No one will understand." But Scripture says we are stronger together. When one falters, another lifts her up (Ecclesiastes 4:9-10).

Healthy Boundaries, Honest Hearts

True connection requires both vulnerability and wisdom. Share your heart, but guard your peace. Not every relationship is meant to go deep, and that's okay.

Being the Friend You Need

Sometimes the best way to find Kingdom community is to become it. Be the woman who shows up, speaks truth in love, prays boldly, and celebrates others without envy.

Journal Moments

1. Who in your life encourages your faith and calls you higher?

2. Where do you need to set boundaries to protect your peace?

3. How can you be a better friend to the women God has placed in your life?

4. Pray: Lord, surround me with Kingdom sisters who sharpen me and celebrate me.

I am not alone. I am supported. I am surrounded by Kingdom community.

Chapter 11 – Financial Stewardship: Managing Resources With Kingdom Vision

"Honor the Lord with your wealth, with the firstfruits of all your crops." – Proverbs 3:9

Money is not the enemy; the love of money is. When managed with Kingdom vision, your finances become a tool for generosity, freedom, and impact. Financial alignment means your spending reflects your values and your giving reflects your worship.

Many women feel shame around money — either for having too little or for wanting more. But God cares about your financial well-being because He knows it affects your peace, your family, and your ability to fulfill His calling.

Scarcity vs. Abundance Mindset

Scarcity says, "There's never enough." Abundance trusts God's provision. When you shift from fear-based financial decisions to faith-based stewardship, generosity flows naturally.

Biblical Principles of Wealth

Scripture is full of financial wisdom:

- Tithe first (Malachi 3:10)

- Live below your means (Proverbs 21:5)

- Avoid debt (Proverbs 22:7)

- Be generous (2 Corinthians 9:7)

Building a Kingdom Budget

Your budget should reflect your priorities. Where does your money go? Does it align with your values? Financial alignment creates peace and positions you to bless others.

Journal Moments

1. What beliefs about money did you inherit from your upbringing?

2. How does your current spending reflect (or not reflect) Kingdom priorities?

3. Where can you increase generosity in your life?

4. Pray: Lord, help me steward my resources wisely and generously.

I am a faithful steward. I am financially free. I am generous with what God provides.

Chapter 12 – Leading From Your Lane: Discovering Your Unique Gifting

"There are different kinds of gifts, but the same Spirit distributes them." – 1 Corinthians 12:4

God didn't create you to be a carbon copy of anyone else. Your gifts, experiences, and calling are uniquely yours. Leading from your lane means embracing what God placed in you without comparison, competition, or compromise.

You don't have to do everything; you just have to do your thing — faithfully, boldly, and with excellence. When you operate in your gifting, ministry feels like worship, not work.

Identifying Your Gifts

Your gifts often show up at the intersection of passion and impact. What do you love to do? What do people say you're naturally good at? Where do you see fruit?

The Danger of Drift

When you step outside your lane to impress others or keep up with trends, you lose effectiveness. Stay rooted in what God called you to do, even if it looks different from everyone else.

Permission to Say No

Saying no to opportunities outside your lane is saying yes to your calling. Boundaries protect your anointing.

Journal Moments

1. What gifts has God placed in you that you've been afraid to use?

2. Where have you drifted into someone else's lane?

3. What would it look like to fully embrace your unique assignment?

4. Pray: Lord, show me my lane and give me courage to stay in it.

I am gifted. I am called. I am confident in my unique assignment.

Chapter 13 — Navigating Transition: Trusting God in the Waiting

"Wait for the Lord; be strong and take heart and wait for the Lord." — Psalm 27:14

Transition is the space between where you were and where you're going. It's uncomfortable, uncertain, and often confusing. But transition is also sacred — it's where transformation happens.

When God moves you from one season to another, He doesn't rush. He uses the waiting to prepare you, prune you, and position you. The question is not "How long?" but "What are You teaching me here, Lord?"

The Wilderness Before the Promise

Every major move of God includes a wilderness season. Moses spent forty years in the desert before leading Israel. David was anointed king but waited years to take the throne. Jesus fasted forty days before beginning His ministry. If they needed preparation, so do you.

Faith in the Fog

Transition often feels like walking through fog — you can only see the next step. That's by design. God wants you to trust Him, not the plan.

Blooming Where You're Planted

While you wait, don't waste the season. Serve where you are. Grow where you're planted. Steward what's in front of you with faithfulness.

Journal Moments

1. What season of transition are you currently in?

2. What is God teaching you in the waiting?

3. How can you stay faithful while trusting His timing?

4. Pray: Lord, help me trust You when I can't see the full picture.

I trust God's timing. I am growing in the waiting. I am being prepared for what's next.

Chapter 14 – Prayer as Partnership: Co-Laboring With God

"Rejoice always, pray continually, give thanks in all circumstances; for this is God's will for you in Christ Jesus." – 1 Thessalonians 5:16-18

Prayer is not a religious obligation; it's an intimate partnership with the Creator of the universe. When you pray, you invite God into every area of your life — your decisions, relationships, struggles, and dreams. Prayer changes things because it changes you.

Too often we treat prayer like a shopping list or emergency hotline. But aligned prayer is conversation, collaboration, and communion. It's how you stay connected to your Source.

Building a Consistent Prayer Life

Consistency doesn't mean perfection. Start small: five minutes in the morning, a prayer over meals, gratitude before bed. Make prayer a rhythm, not a ritual.

Praying God's Word

When you don't know what to pray, pray Scripture. God's Word is alive and active. Declare His promises over your life, your family, and your calling.

Listening, Not Just Talking

Prayer is two-way communication. Spend time in silence, listening for God's still, small voice. He speaks through Scripture, through peace, through confirmation, and through others.

Journal Moments

1. How would you describe your current prayer life?

2. What keeps you from praying consistently?

3. Write a prayer declaring God's promises over your current season.

4. Pray: Lord, teach me to pray in a way that draws me closer to You.

I am a woman of prayer. I am heard by God. I am partnered with Heaven.

Chapter 15 – Mental Wellness: Renewing the Mind Daily

"Do not conform to the pattern of this world, but be transformed by the renewing of your mind." – Romans 12:2

Your mind is a battlefield, and mental wellness is a spiritual discipline. Anxiety, depression, stress, and overwhelm are real struggles, but they don't have to define you. God invites you to renew your mind daily with His truth.

Mental wellness includes therapy, rest, boundaries, community, and Scripture. It's holistic care for the mind God gave you. You can honor Him by stewarding your mental health well.

Identifying Thought Patterns

Negative thought patterns often run on autopilot. Awareness is the first step toward change. What narratives play on repeat in your mind? Are they true? Are they kind? Are they from God?

Taking Thoughts Captive

2 Corinthians 10:5 tells us to "take captive every thought to make it obedient to Christ." That means intentionally interrupting destructive thinking and replacing it with truth.

The Role of Professional Help

Therapy is not a lack of faith; it's wise stewardship. God uses counselors, doctors, and mental health professionals as part of His healing plan. Don't be afraid to get the help you need.

Journal Moments

1. What recurring thoughts steal your peace?

2. How can you practice taking thoughts captive this week?

3. What support (therapy, community, rest) do you need to prioritize your mental wellness?

4. Pray: Lord, renew my mind and guard my heart with Your peace.

I am mentally strong. I am emotionally healthy. I am renewed by God's truth daily.

Chapter 16 – Forgiveness as Freedom: Releasing What Holds You Back

"Bear with each other and forgive one another if any of you has a grievance against someone. Forgive as the Lord forgave you." – Colossians 3:13

Unforgiveness is a prison you build for yourself. It keeps you chained to the past, replaying hurt, and rehearsing bitterness. But forgiveness is the key that sets you free — not for the other person's sake, but for yours.

Forgiveness doesn't mean what happened was okay. It means you refuse to let it define your future. When you release the debt, you release the weight.

The Cost of Holding On

Unforgiveness affects your body, mind, and spirit. It breeds resentment, steals joy, and blocks your ability to receive God's peace. Holding a grudge is like drinking poison and expecting the other person to die.

Forgiving Yourself

Sometimes the hardest person to forgive is yourself. But God's grace covers your past mistakes, poor choices, and failures. If He has forgiven you, who are you to withhold forgiveness from yourself?

The Process, Not Perfection

Forgiveness is not a one-time decision; it's a daily choice. Some days you'll have to forgive the same person (or yourself) repeatedly. That's okay. Keep choosing freedom.

Journal Moments

1. Who do you need to forgive, and what is holding you back?

2. How has unforgiveness affected your peace or relationships?

3. Write a prayer releasing someone (or yourself) from the debt of hurt.

4. Pray: Lord, help me forgive as You have forgiven me.

I am free. I am forgiven. I release what no longer serves me.

Chapter 17 – Legacy Living: Building Something That Outlasts You

"A good person leaves an inheritance for their children's children." – Proverbs 13:22

Your life is more than the years you live; it's the impact you leave behind. Legacy is not about fame or fortune — it's about the values you instill, the love you give, and the faith you pass on.

Every woman leaves a legacy, whether intentional or not. The question is: what will yours be? Will those who come after you know that you loved God, served others, and walked in purpose?

Living With the End in Mind

When you consider how you want to be remembered, it clarifies how you should live today. What do you want said about you? What do you want your life to stand for?

Investing in Others

Legacy is built through relationships. Mentor younger women. Share your wisdom. Speak life into the next generation. Your influence multiplies when you pour into others.

Leaving a Spiritual Inheritance

The greatest legacy you can leave is faith. When your children, grandchildren, or spiritual daughters see your unwavering trust in God, they inherit more than money — they inherit hope.

Journal Moments

1. How do you want to be remembered?

2. What values are you currently passing on to those around you?

3. Who can you invest in or mentor in this season?

4. Pray: Lord, help me live a life that leaves a legacy of faith, love, and purpose.

I am building a legacy. I am living with intention. I am leaving an inheritance of faith.

Chapter 18 – Joy as Resistance: Choosing Gladness in Hard Seasons

"The joy of the Lord is your strength." – Nehemiah 8:10

Joy is not the absence of hardship; it's the defiant choice to trust God in the midst of it. When circumstances try to steal your peace, joy becomes an act of spiritual resistance. It declares, "God is still good, and I will still praise Him."

Happiness depends on circumstances; joy depends on Jesus. You can be sorrowful yet always rejoicing (2 Corinthians 6:10). This is the mystery and power of Kingdom joy.

Finding Joy in Small Things

Joy is not always loud or dramatic. Sometimes it's quiet gratitude for a sunrise, a kind word, or a moment of peace. Train your heart to notice goodness, even in hard seasons.

Guarding Your Joy

Comparison, complaining, and bitterness erode joy. Protect it by practicing gratitude, speaking life, and choosing hope over despair.

Joy as a Witness

Your joy in hardship is a testimony to the world. It points people to the Source of your strength. When you choose joy, you shine light into darkness.

Journal Moments

1. What steals your joy most often?

2. Where can you find gratitude in your current season?

3. How can choosing joy become an act of worship?

4. Pray: Lord, fill me with Your joy, even when circumstances challenge me.

I choose joy. I choose gratitude. I choose to trust God in every season.

Chapter 19 – Finishing Strong: Faithful to the End

"I have fought the good fight, I have finished the race, I have kept the faith." – 2 Timothy 4:7

The goal is not just to start well, but to finish well. Many begin with passion, but aligned women sustain through perseverance. Finishing strong requires endurance, faithfulness, and a refusal to quit when the road gets hard.

God is not impressed by flash; He honors follow-through. When you commit to living aligned, stewarding your gifts, and walking in obedience, you position yourself to cross the finish line with confidence.

Endurance Over Intensity

The Christian life is a marathon, not a sprint. Pace yourself. Rest when needed. Keep showing up, even on the days you don't feel like it.

Course Corrections Are Normal

Finishing strong doesn't mean you never stumble. It means you get back up, realign, and keep moving forward. Grace covers the journey.

The Crown Awaits

When you finish your race faithfully, a crown of righteousness awaits (2 Timothy 4:8). Your obedience matters. Your endurance counts. God sees every faithful step.

Journal Moments

1. What race has God called you to run?

2. Where do you need endurance right now?

3. How can you pace yourself for long-term faithfulness?

4. Pray: Lord, give me strength to finish strong and run my race with joy.

I am enduring. I am faithful. I am finishing strong in the power of Christ.

Afterword – The Commissioning

When you began this journey, perhaps you weren't sure who you were or what God was calling you to do next. Now you stand on new ground — aware, awakened, and aligned.

This isn't the end; it's the beginning of a new way of living. Step forward with courage. Your story is God's platform for His glory.

"See, I am doing a new thing! Now it springs up; do you not perceive it?" – Isaiah 43:19

Receive this commissioning: You are a Kingdom woman — called, equipped, and unshakable. Go live what you've learned.

Reference – The Aligned Woman "I Am" Declarations

1. I am a beloved daughter of God.

2. I am chosen and set apart for purpose.

3. I am whole and healed through Christ.

4. I am strong in the Lord and confident in my calling.

5. I am a voice of faith and hope for others.

6. I am aligned with God's will and walking in peace.

7. I am courageous and compassionate.

8. I am fruitful and faithful in every season.

9. I am anointed to lead, to love, and to shine.

10. I am a Kingdom Aligned Woman — realigned, rediscovered, empowered to lead.

Study Guide & Discussion Questions

Chapter 1 – Identity Reset: Who Am I Now?

Scripture Focus: "Before I formed you in the womb I knew you." — Jeremiah 1:5

1. What past roles or labels have shaped how you see yourself?

2. How does knowing that God formed and knew you before birth redefine your worth?

3. What areas of your identity is God restoring in this new season?

4. How does rediscovering who you are in Christ affect your confidence?

5. Write one declaration of who you are becoming through Him.

Prayer Focus: Lord, help me see myself through Your eyes—whole, chosen, and complete.

Chapter 2 – Core Values & Alignment: Living What Matters Most

Scripture Focus: "But seek first the kingdom of God and His righteousness, and all these things will be added to you." — Matthew 6:33

1. What values guide your decisions today?

2. In what ways do your current priorities reflect (or drift from) God's plan?

3. What does it mean for you personally to "seek first the Kingdom"?

4. How can aligning your faith and daily actions bring peace?

5. What adjustments could you make this week to live in greater alignment?

Prayer Focus: Father, align my heart with Your will so that my life reflects Your Kingdom priorities.

Chapter 3 – Emotional Intelligence & Healing: Mastering the Inner Dialogue

Scripture Focus: "Above all else, guard your heart, for everything you do flows from it." — Proverbs 4:23

1. What emotions tend to dominate your inner voice?

2. How do those feelings shape your relationships and reactions?

3. Where is God inviting you to heal emotionally?

4. What helps you release negative self-talk or unforgiveness?

5. How can you use emotional awareness to walk in peace?

Prayer Focus: Lord, heal my heart and transform my inner dialogue so that my emotions honor You.

Chapter 4 – Confidence & Voice: Speaking Life

Scripture Focus: "The tongue has the power of life and death." — Proverbs 18:21

1. What words have shaped your self-belief over the years?

2. How do you use your voice to encourage or empower others?

3. In what ways can your words align more closely with God's truth?

4. What fear holds you back from speaking boldly?

5. Write one statement of faith you will speak daily.

Prayer Focus: God, fill my heart with courage and my mouth with words of life.

Chapter 5 – Purpose & Next Chapter: Becoming Who You're Called to Be

Scripture Focus: "For we are God's handiwork, created in Christ Jesus to do good works, which God prepared in advance for us to do." — Ephesians 2:10

1. What unique gifts has God placed in you for this season?

2. How do you sense Him calling you to serve or create impact?

3. What distractions or doubts keep you from stepping forward?

4. How can obedience in small steps prepare you for bigger purpose?

5. What does living "on purpose" look like for you right now?

Prayer Focus: Lord, reveal the next step of purpose You've already prepared for me.

Chapter 6 – Integration & Activation: Living Aligned

Scripture Focus: "Let your light shine before others, that they may see your good deeds and glorify your Father in heaven." — Matthew 5:16

1. How has your understanding of alignment changed through this journey?

2. What daily practices help you stay spiritually centered?

3. How can your faith show through your leadership and lifestyle?

4. What does living "unshakable" mean to you personally?

5. How can you shine light in your circle of influence today?

Prayer Focus: Father, let my life reflect Your light and purpose in every action I take.

Group Reflection & Next Steps

Theme: Stepping Into Your Commissioning Circle

- What transformation have you experienced through this journey?

- How has your faith or identity been strengthened?

- In what new way will you walk aligned with God's purpose?

Declaration: I am aligned with purpose, grounded in faith, and unshakable in my walk with God.

Next Step: Write one action you will take this month to live out your alignment. Share it with your community, group, or mentor. Join The Axis North 4 Week or 6 Week Kingdom Aligned Woman classes. Register at www.AxisNorth.org

Made in the USA
Middletown, DE
08 December 2025

22515738R00029